I0472651

Asshole Happen!

Mantras Swear Words

for Realease your Stress away

By

S.B. Nozaz

Copyright © 2016 by S.B. Nozaz

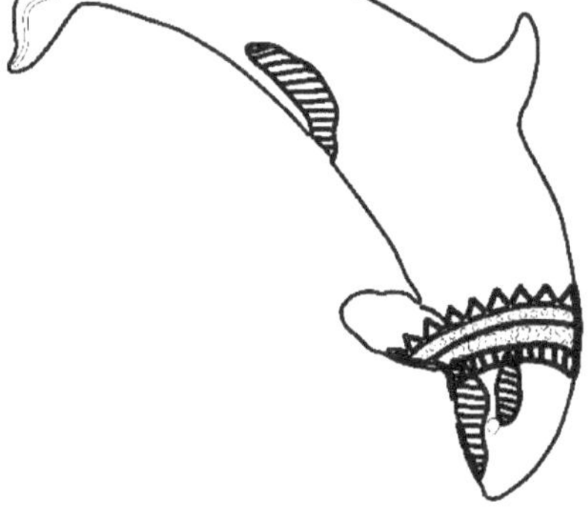

Happy Coloring!

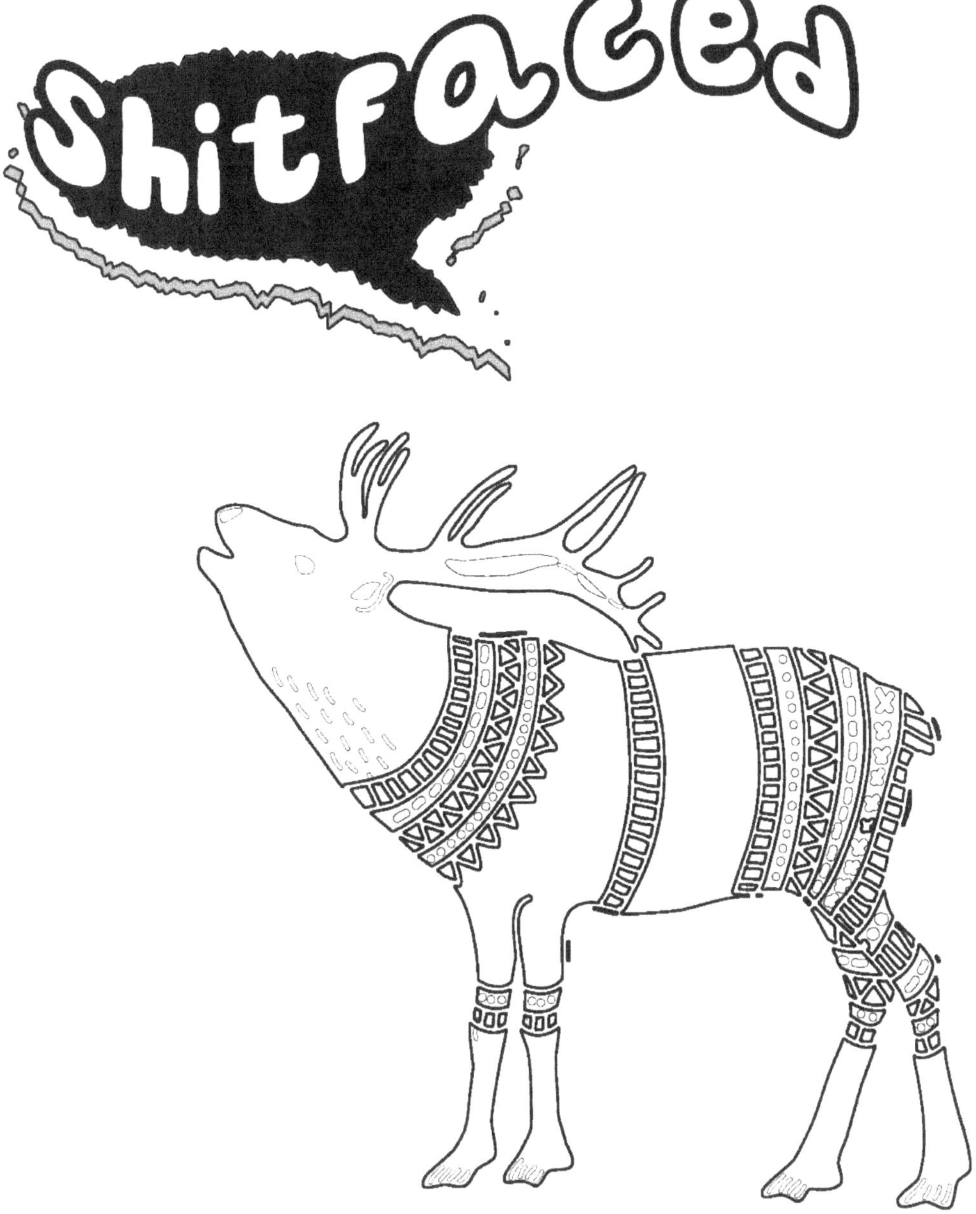
Shitfaced

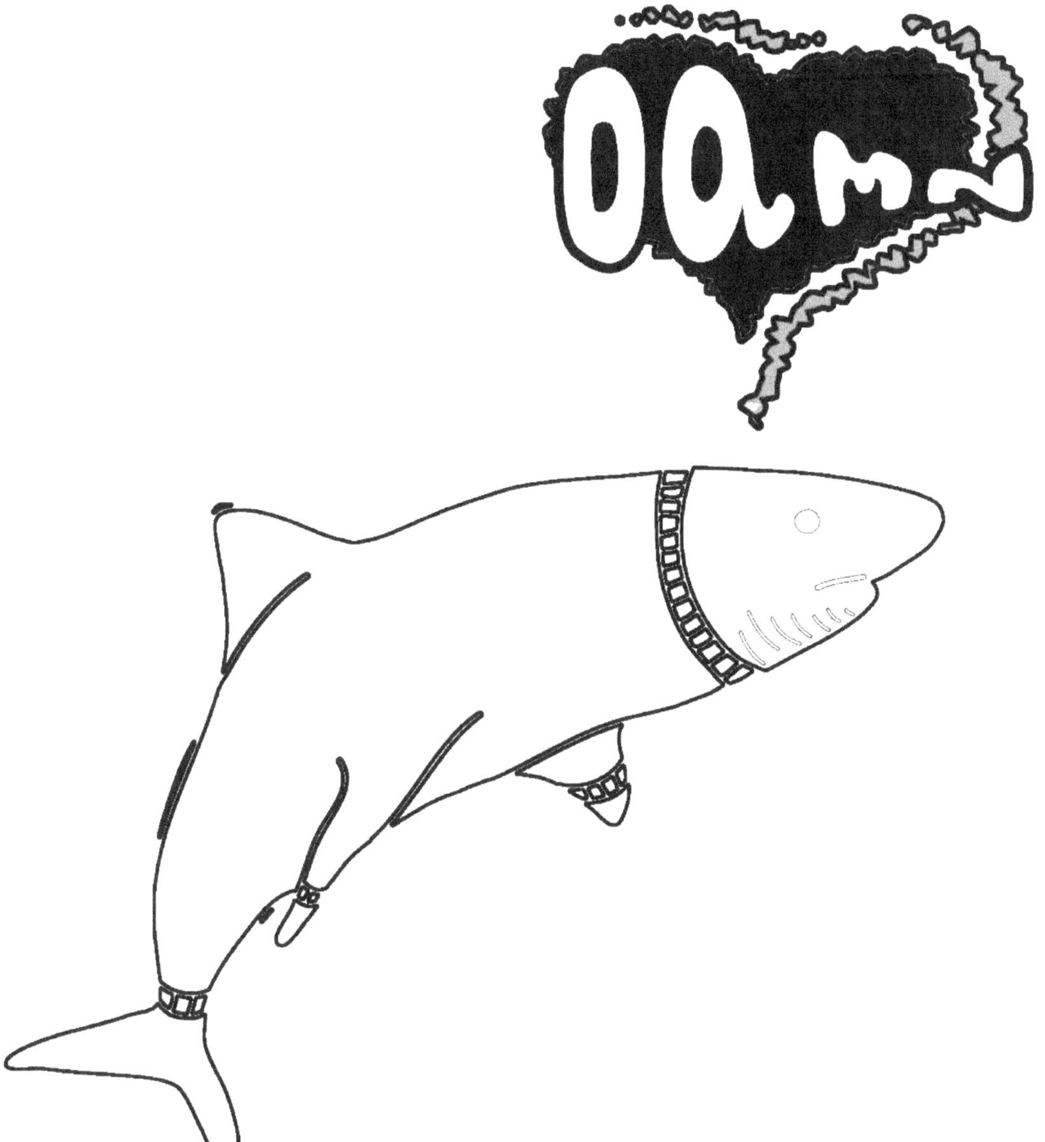

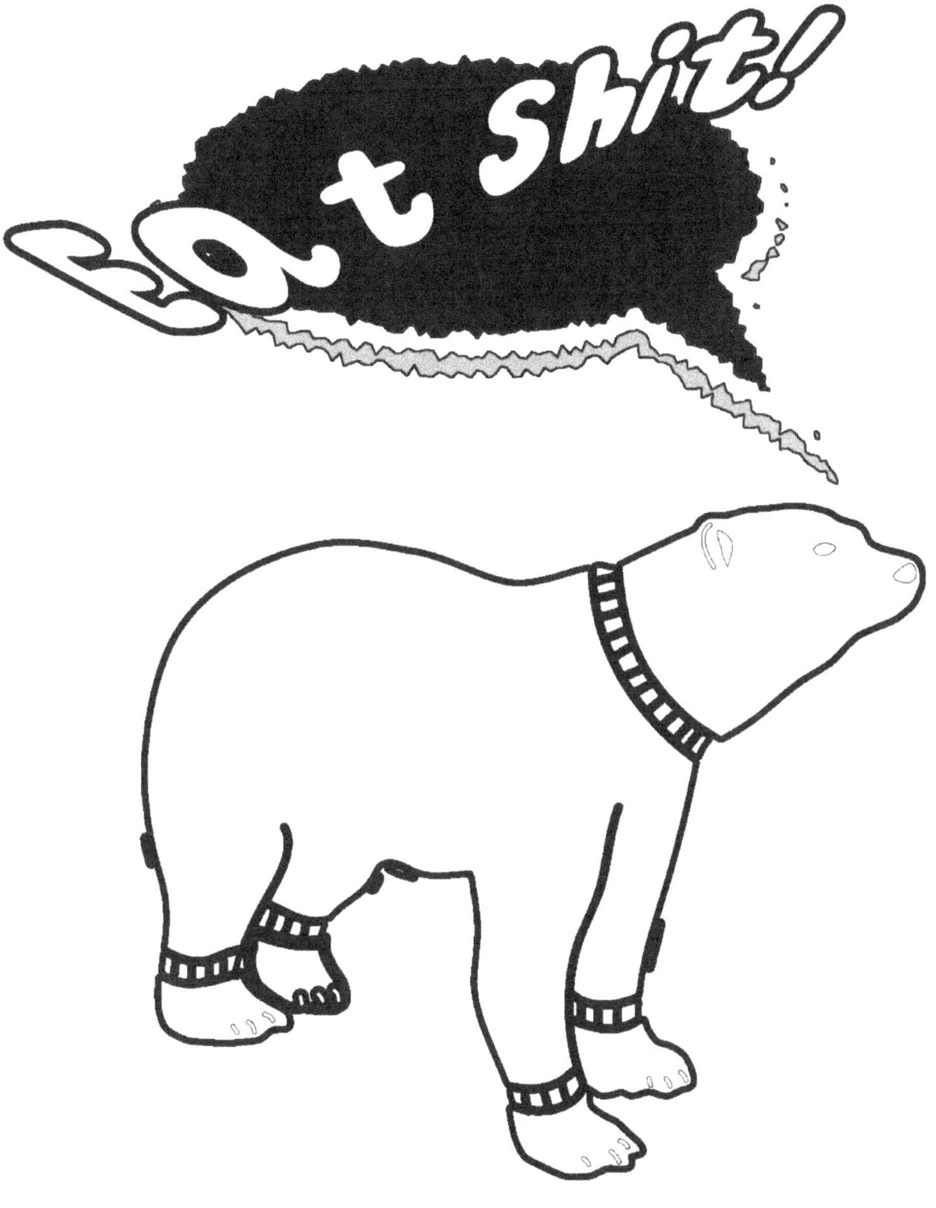
Bat Shit!

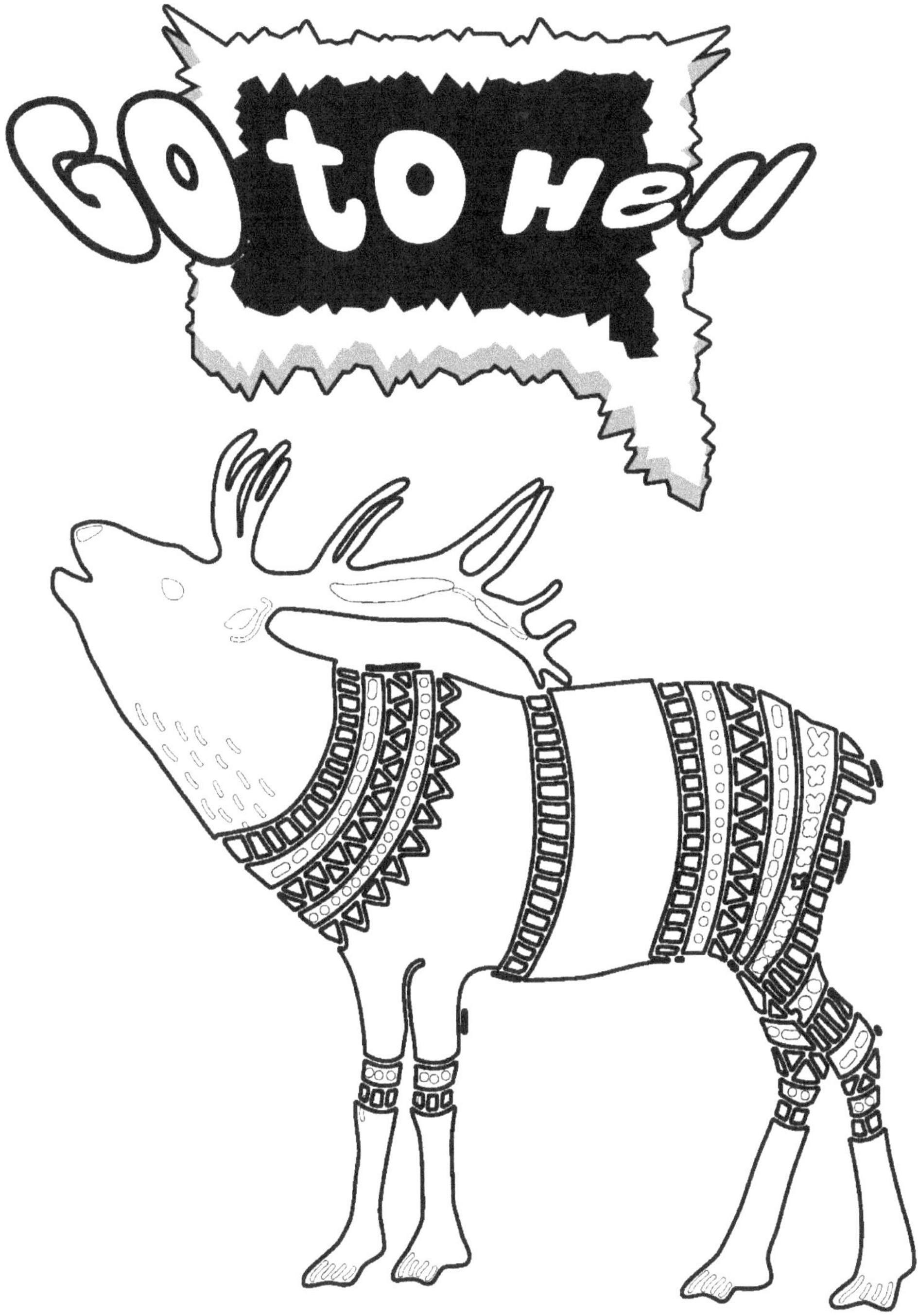
GO to Hell

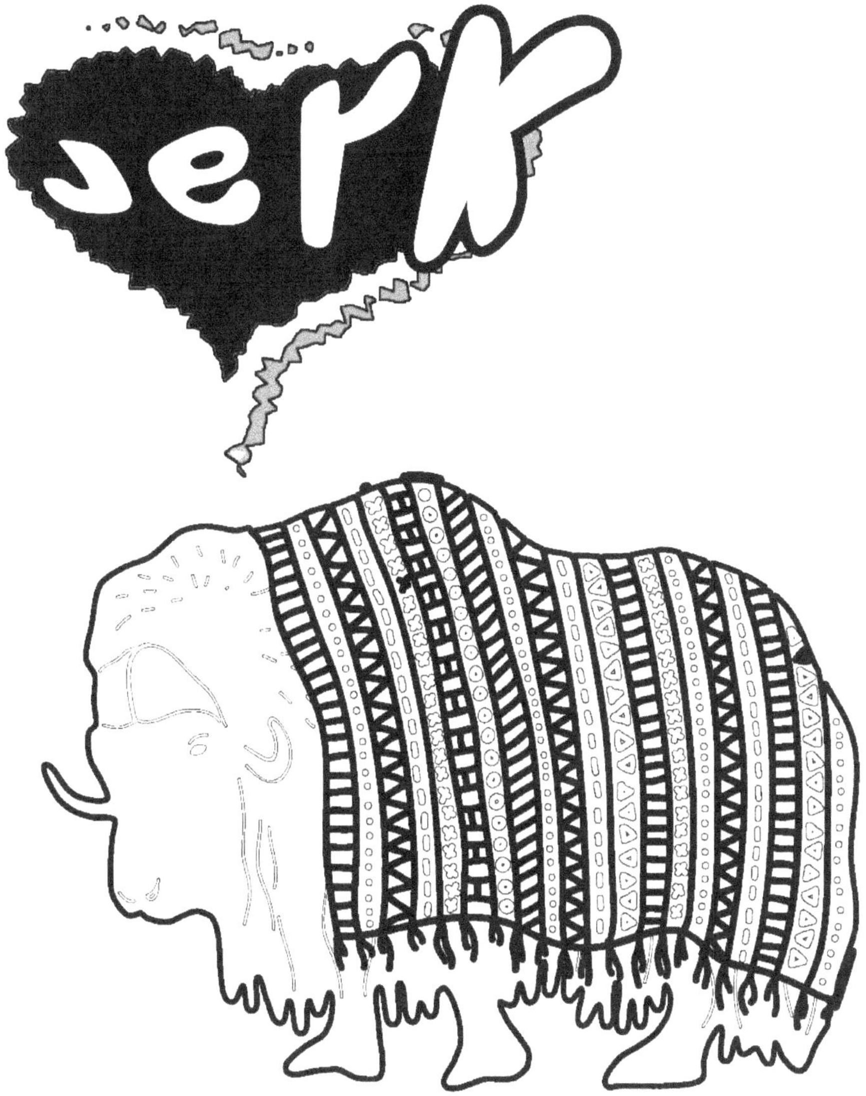
Jerk

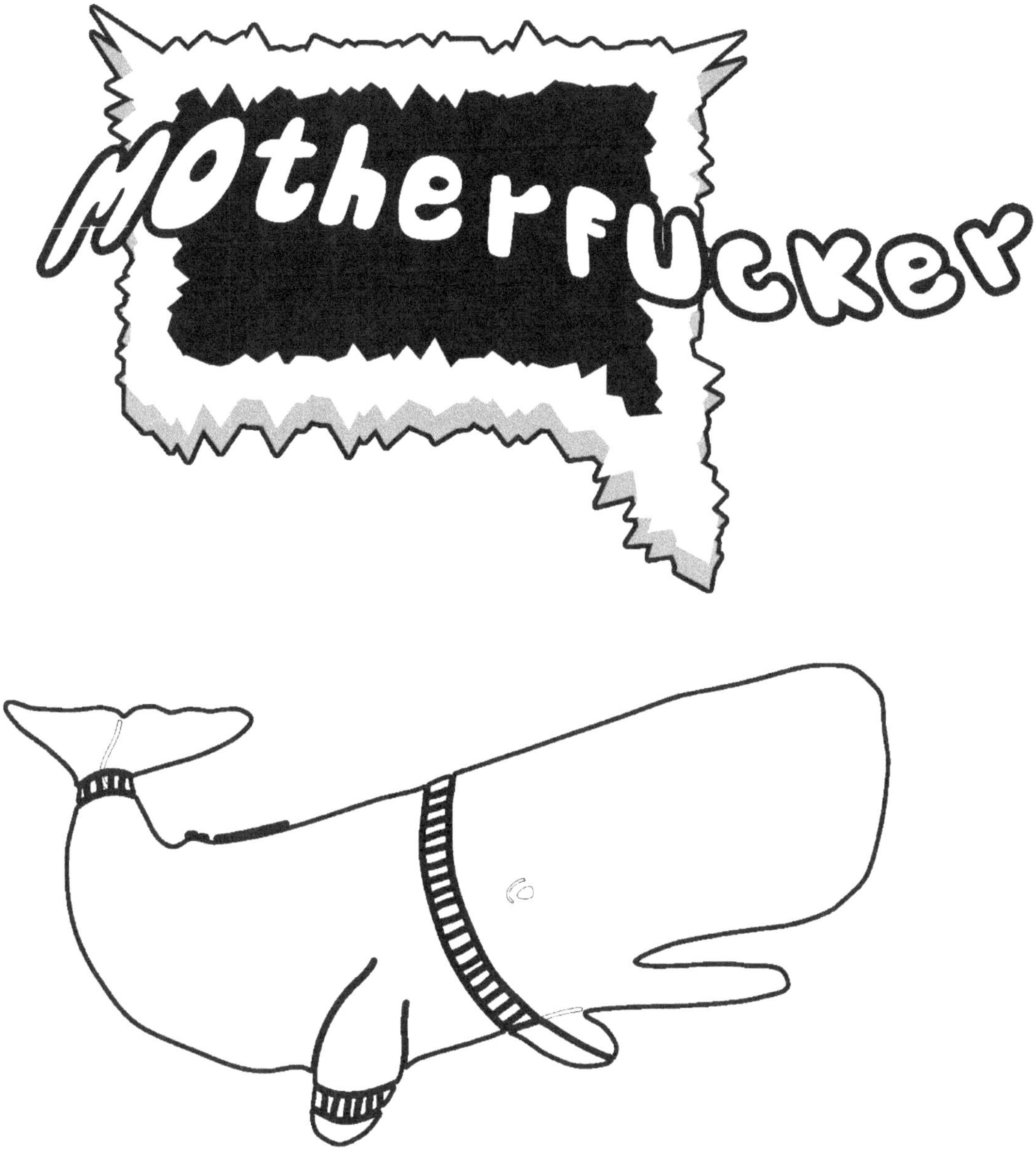
MOtherFUcker

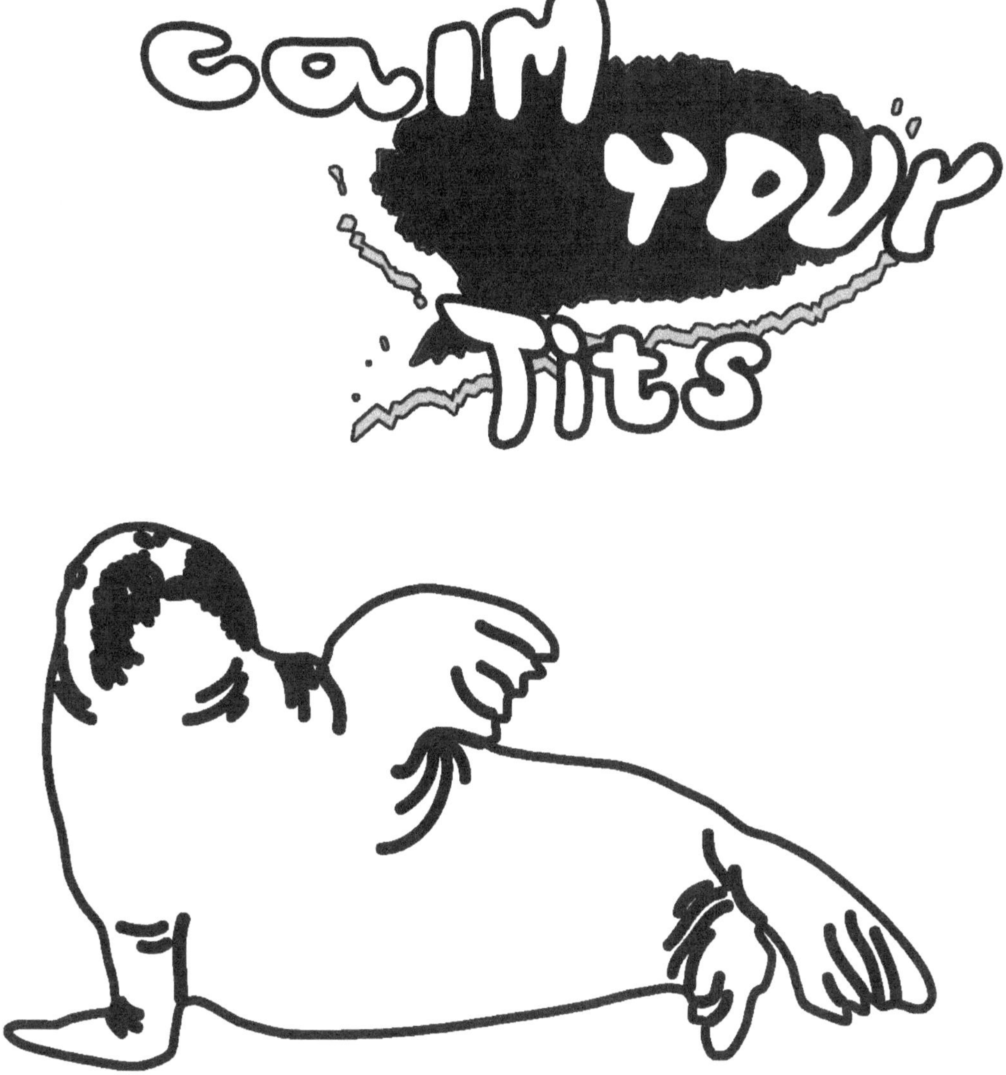
calm your
Tits

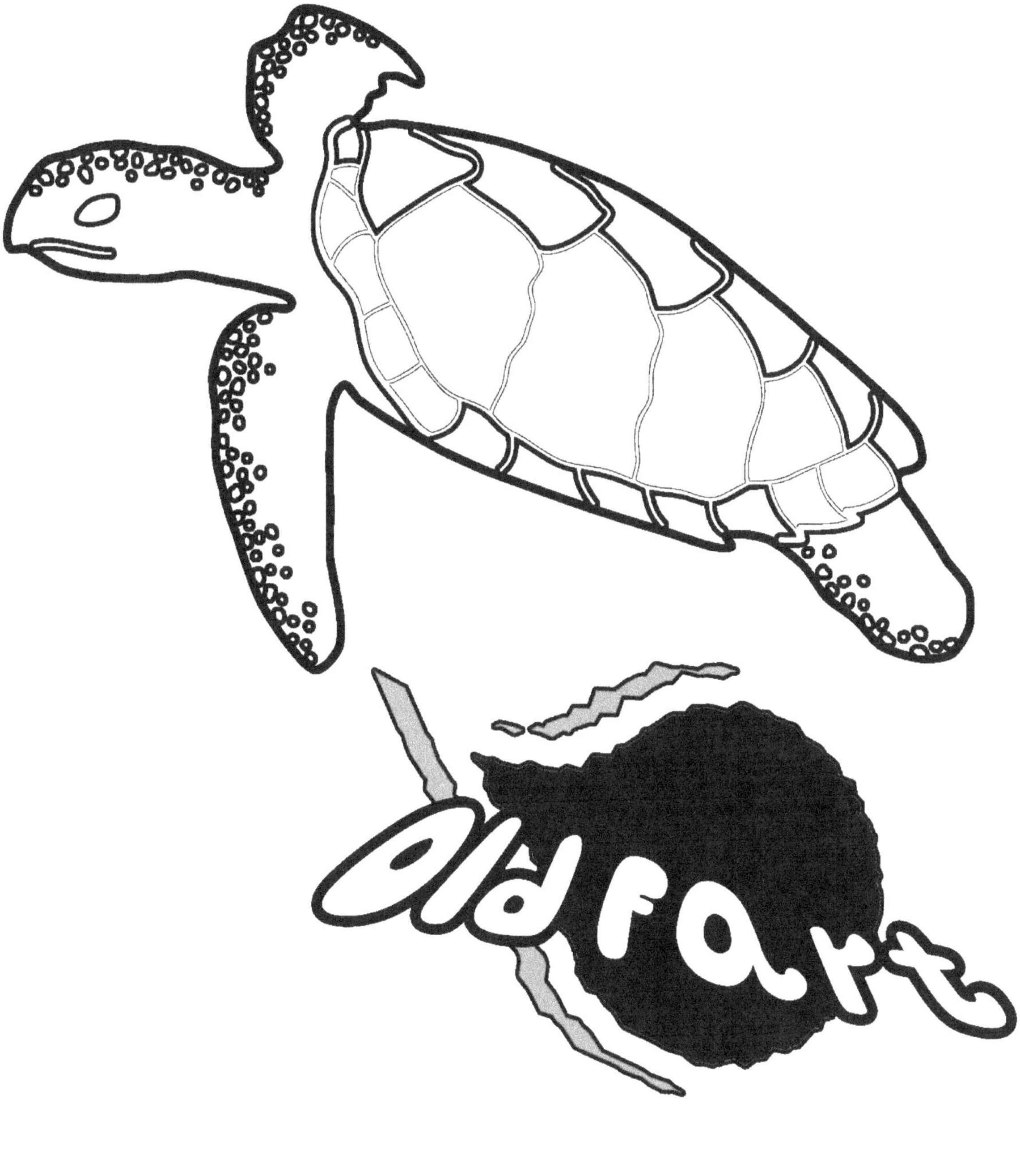
old fart

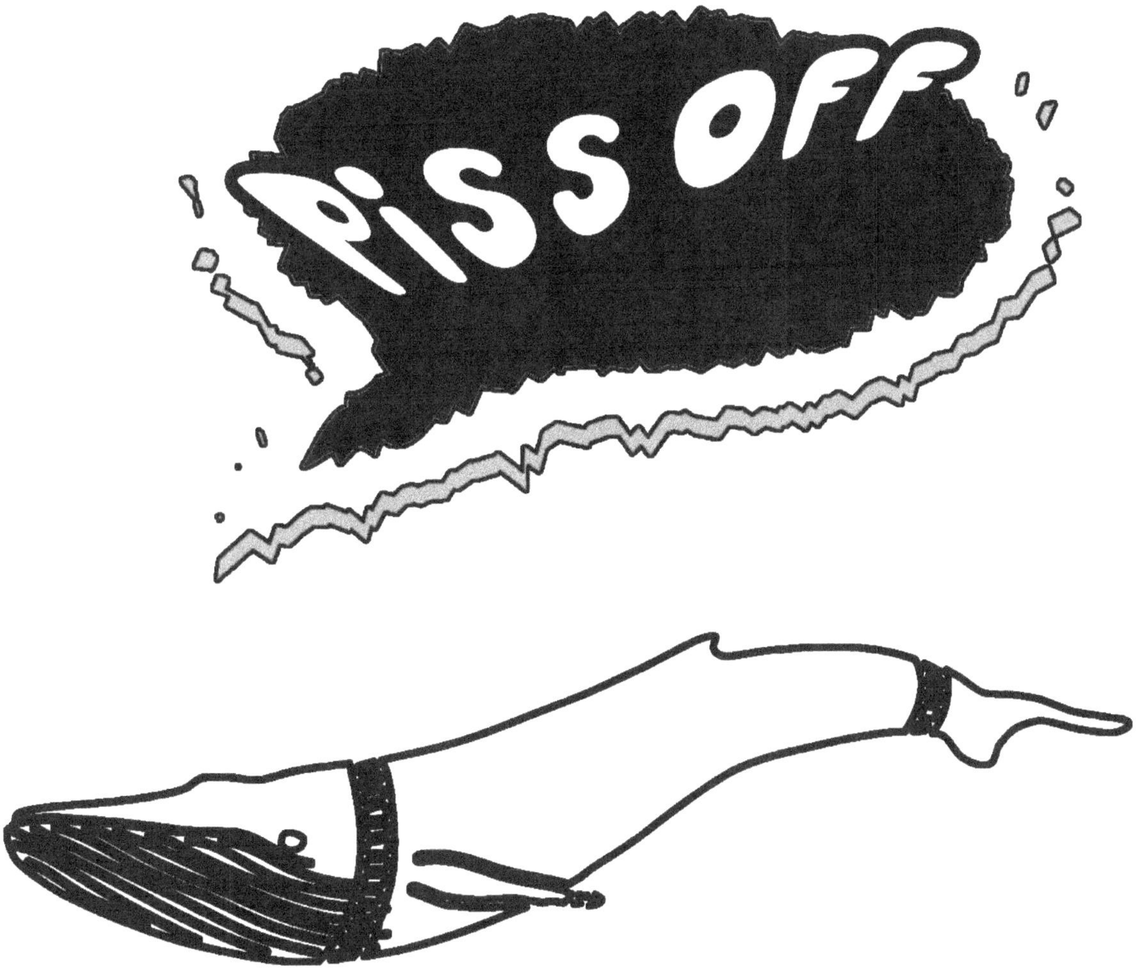
PISS OFF

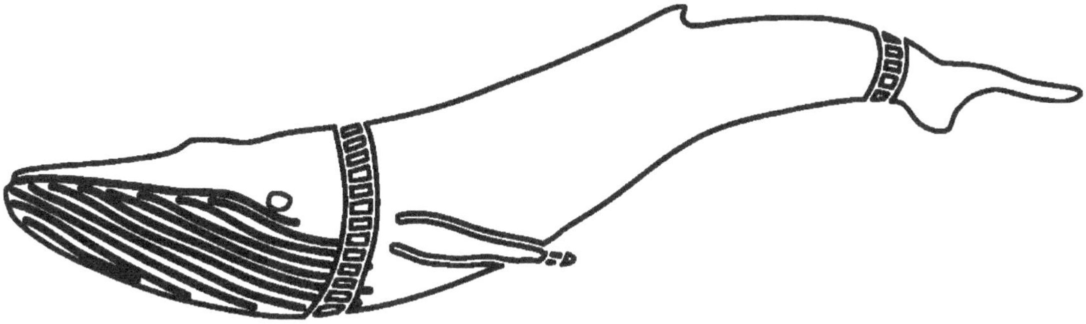

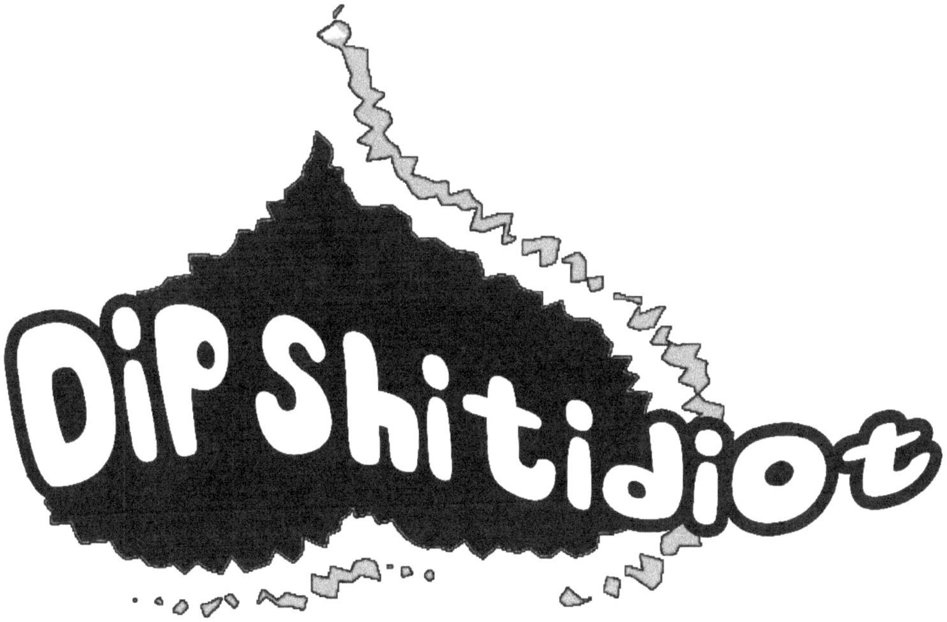
DiP Shitidiot

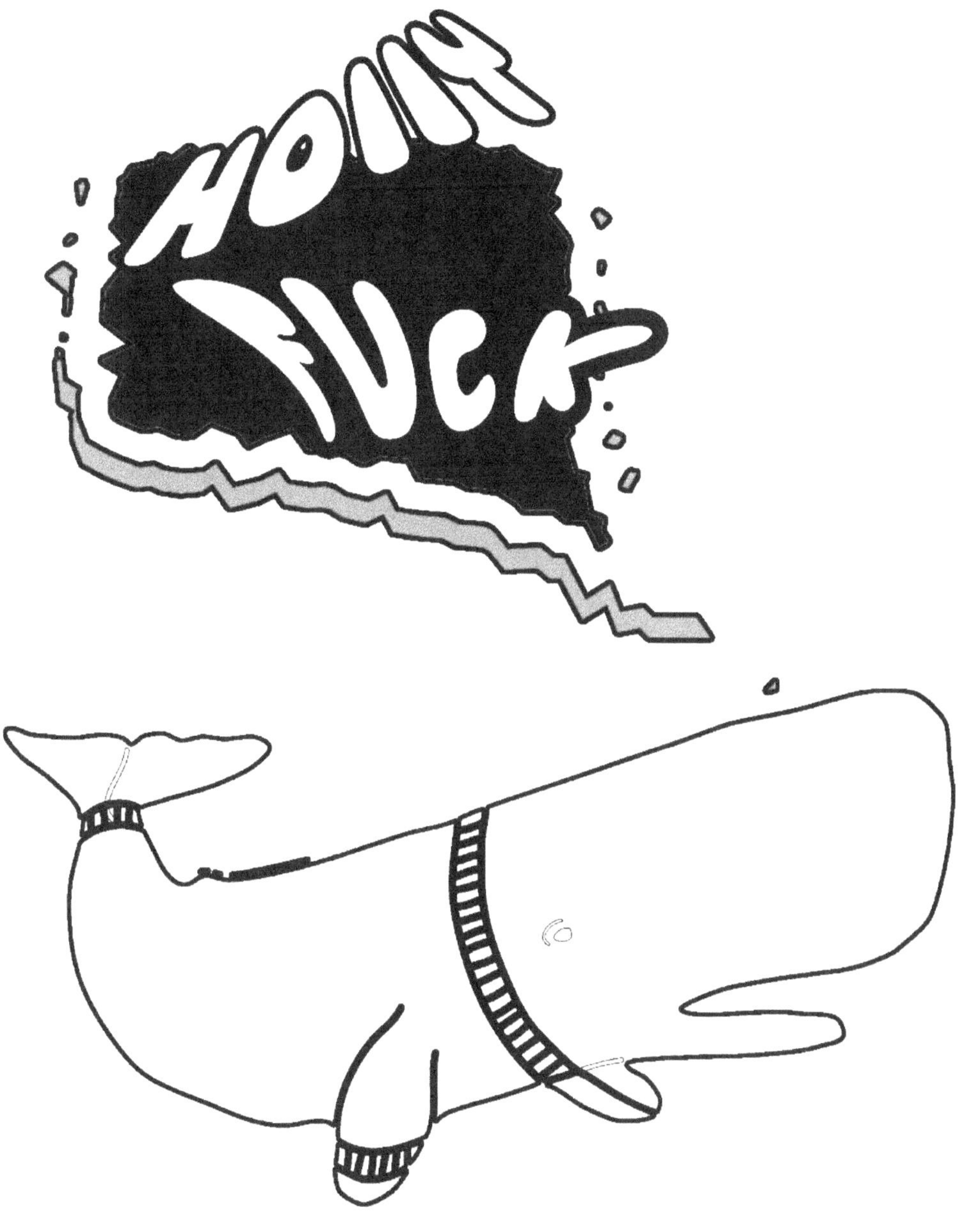
HOLY FUCK

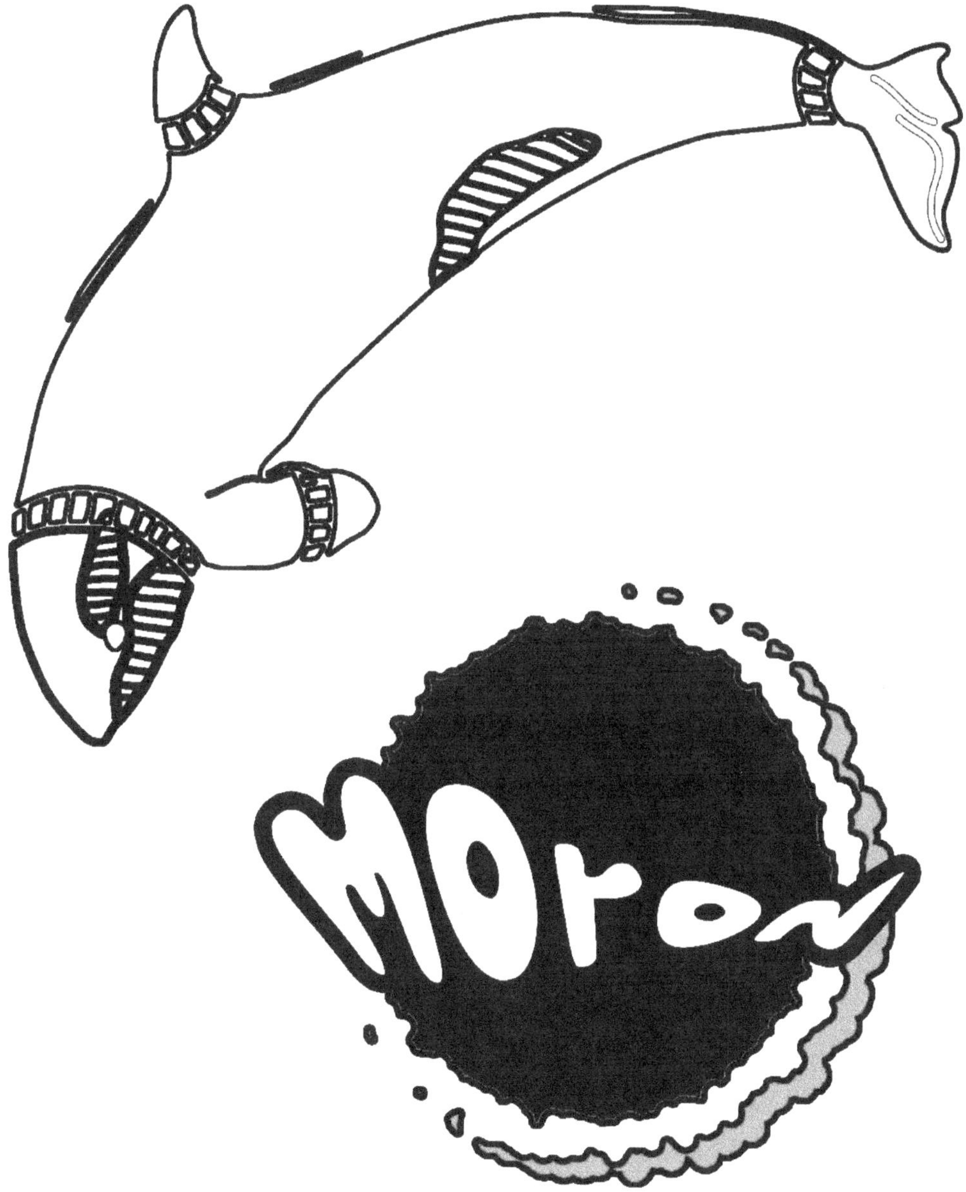
MOron

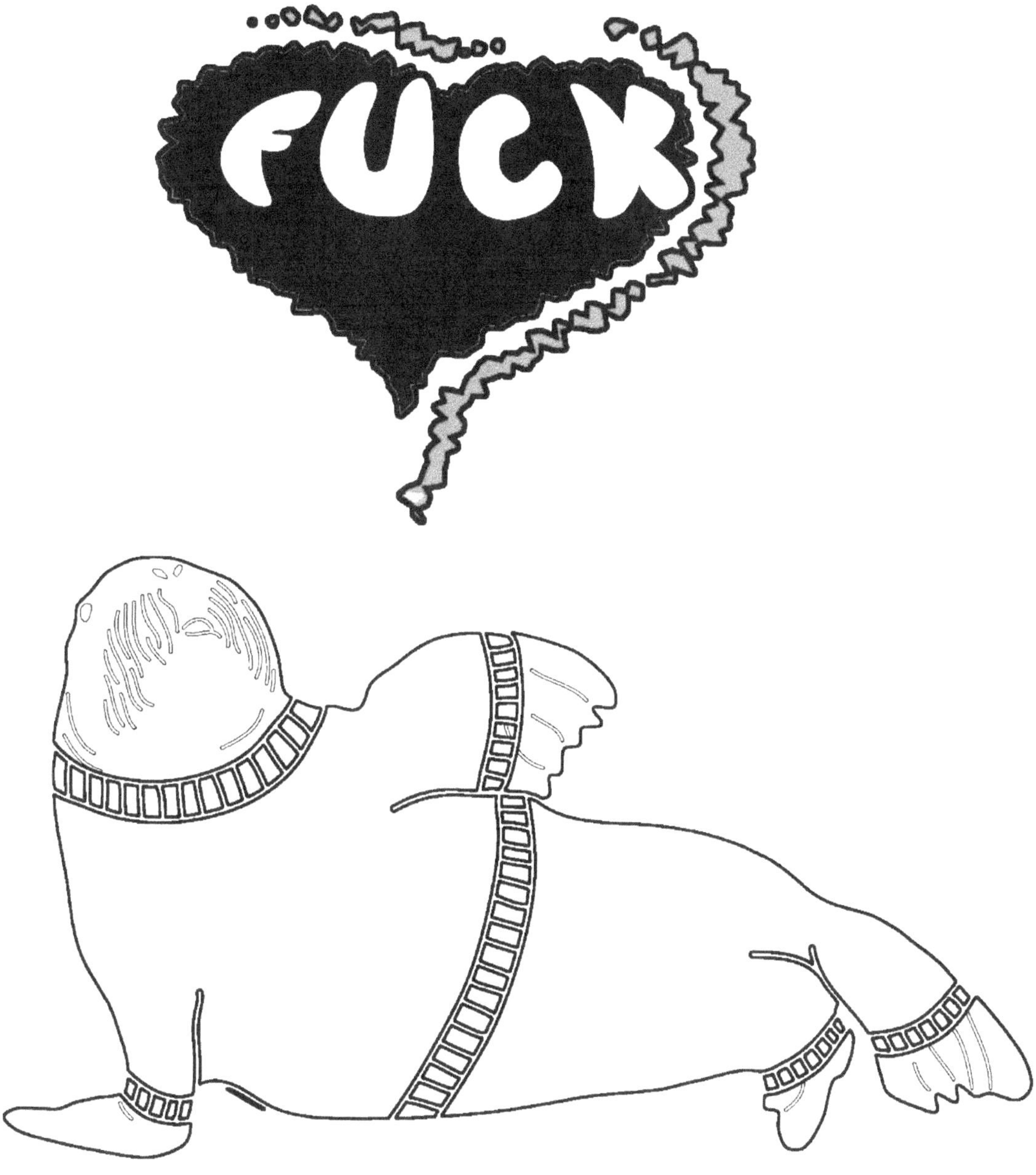
FUCK

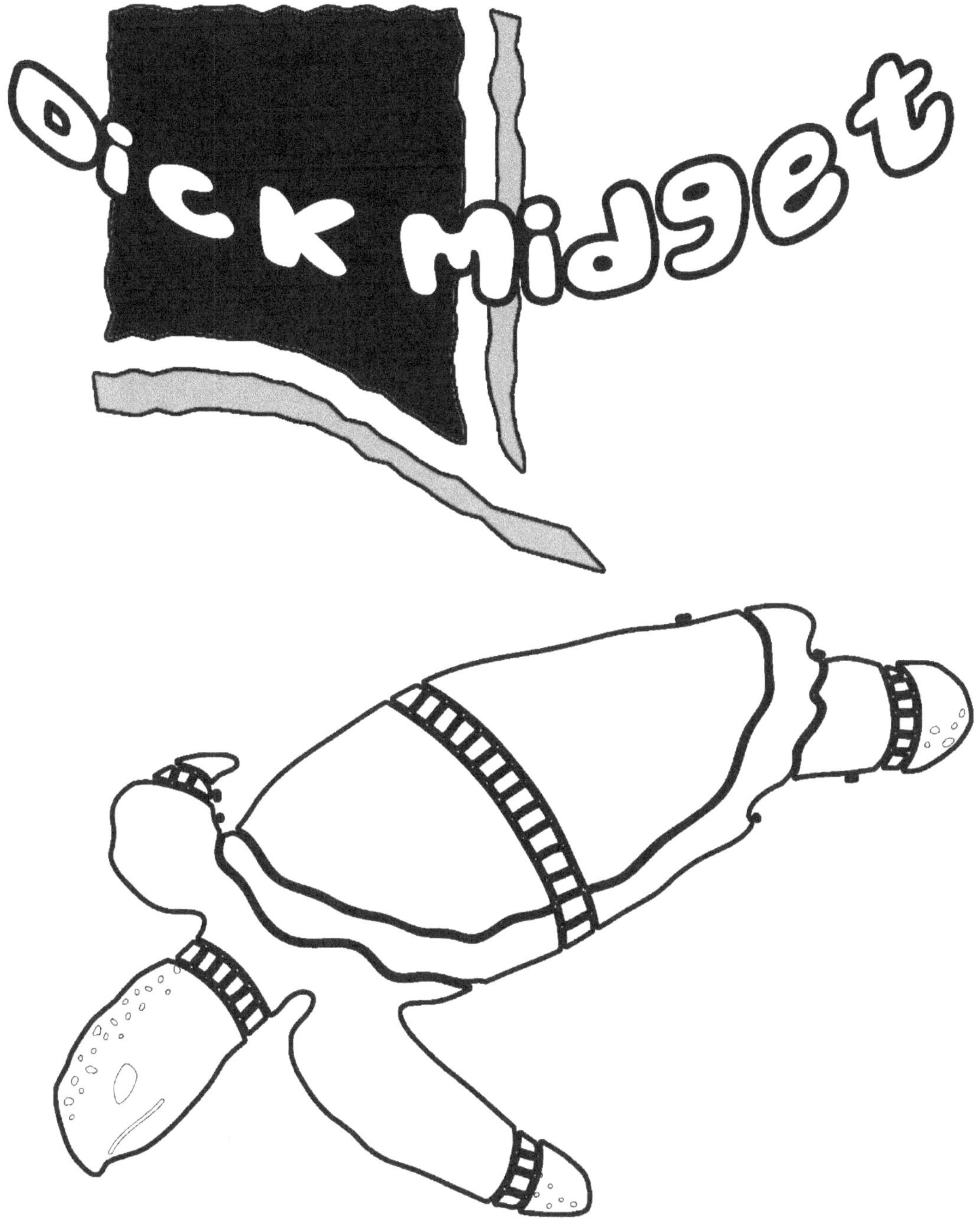
Dick Midget

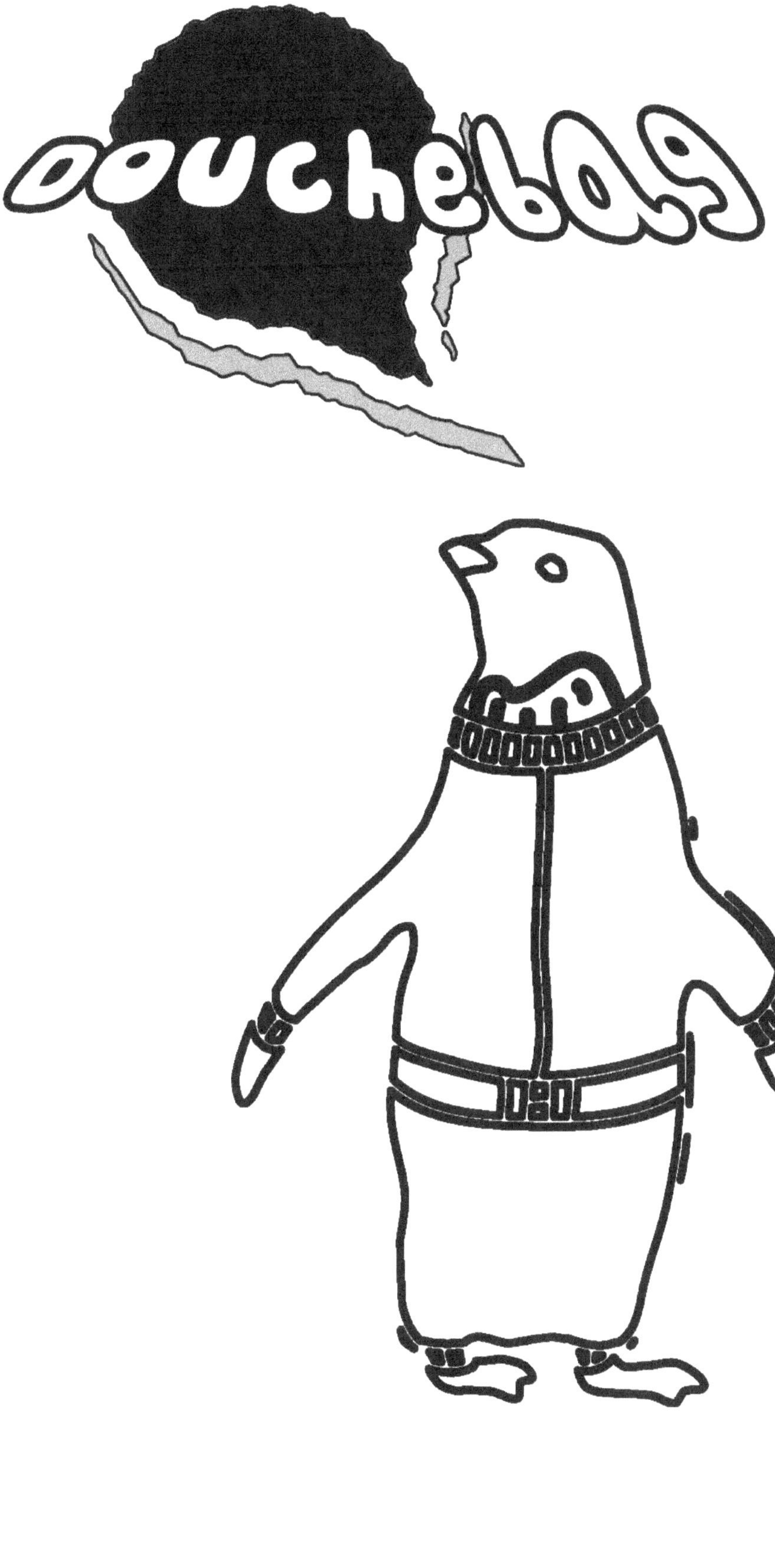
douchebag

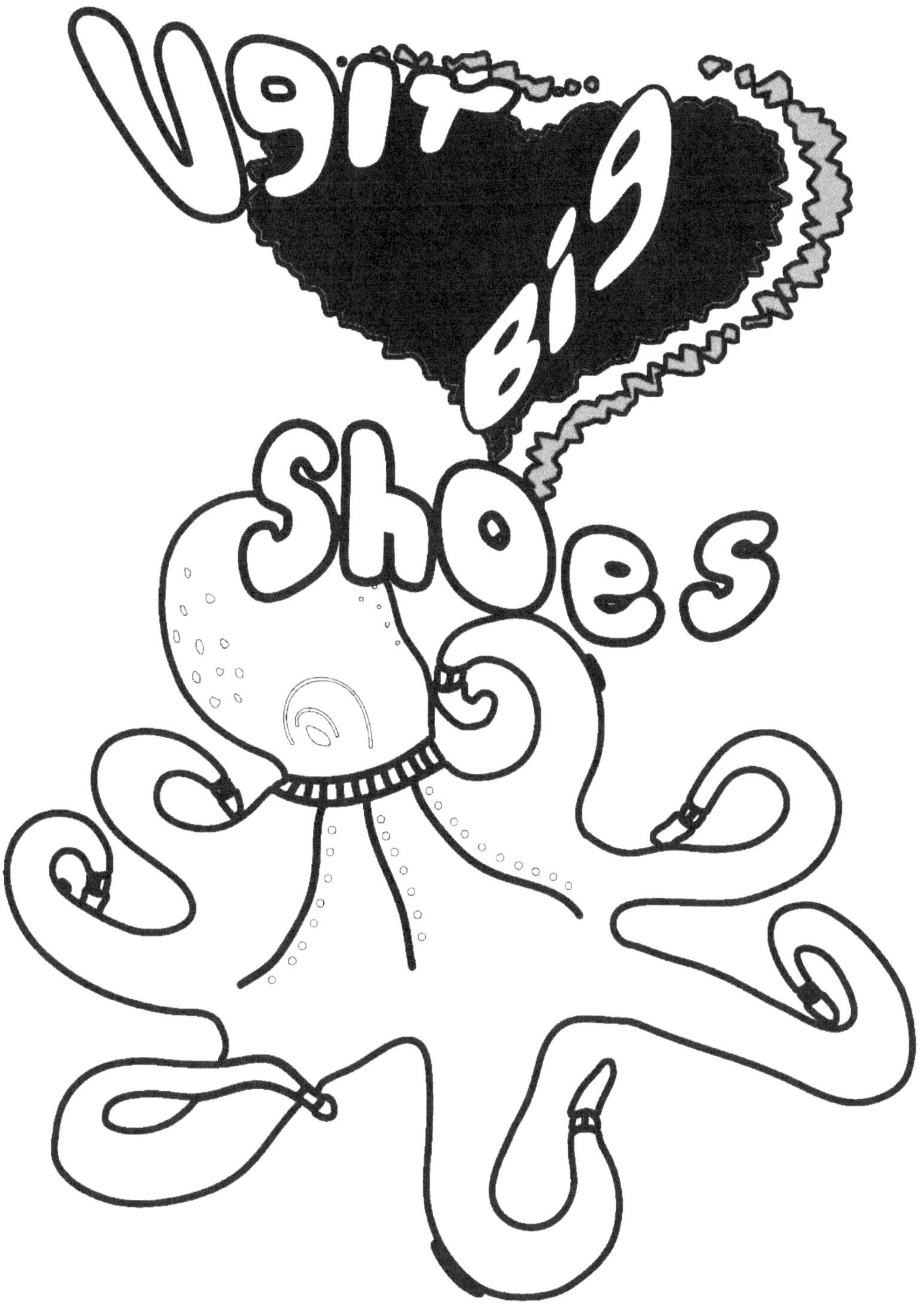
Big
Shoes

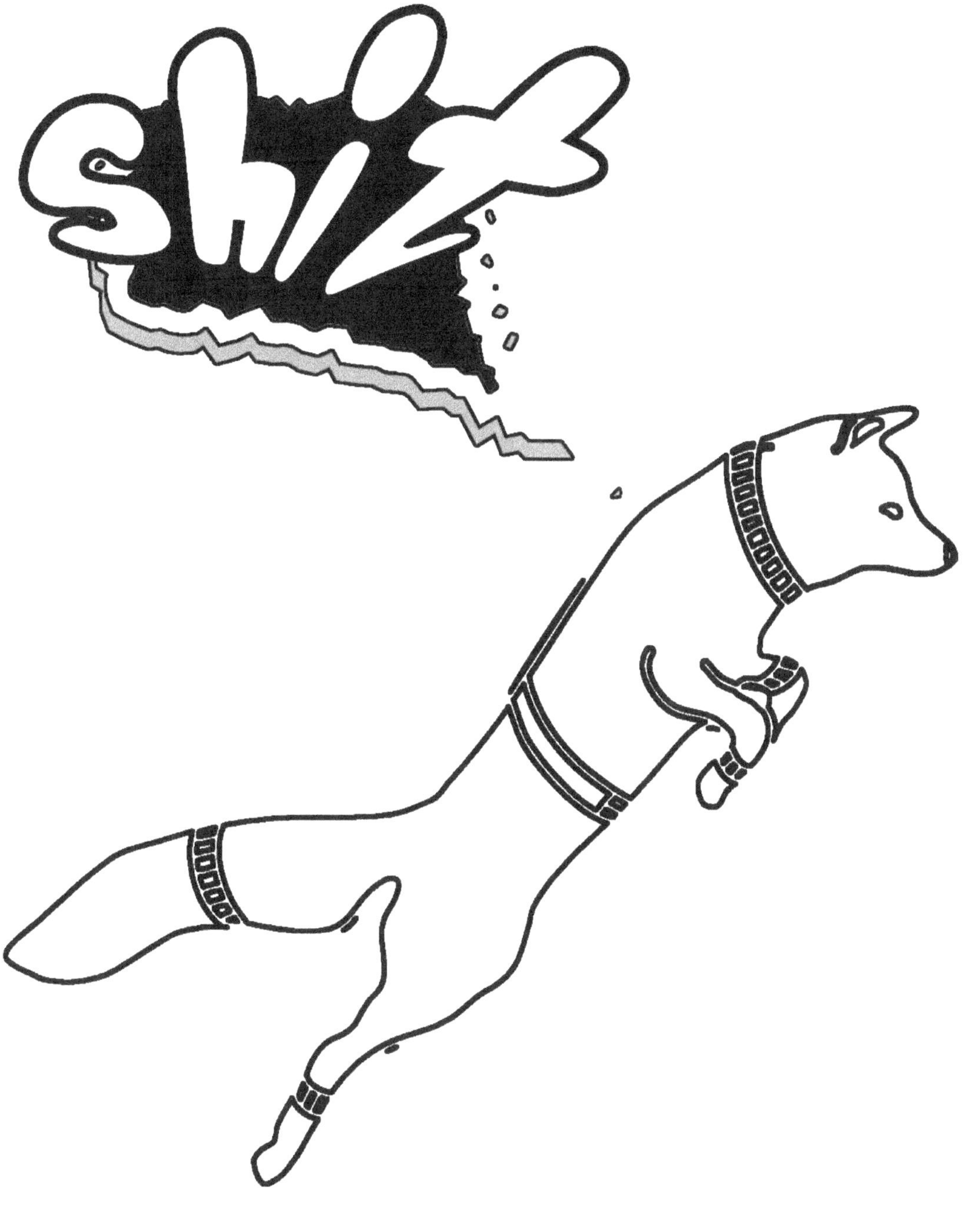
Shit

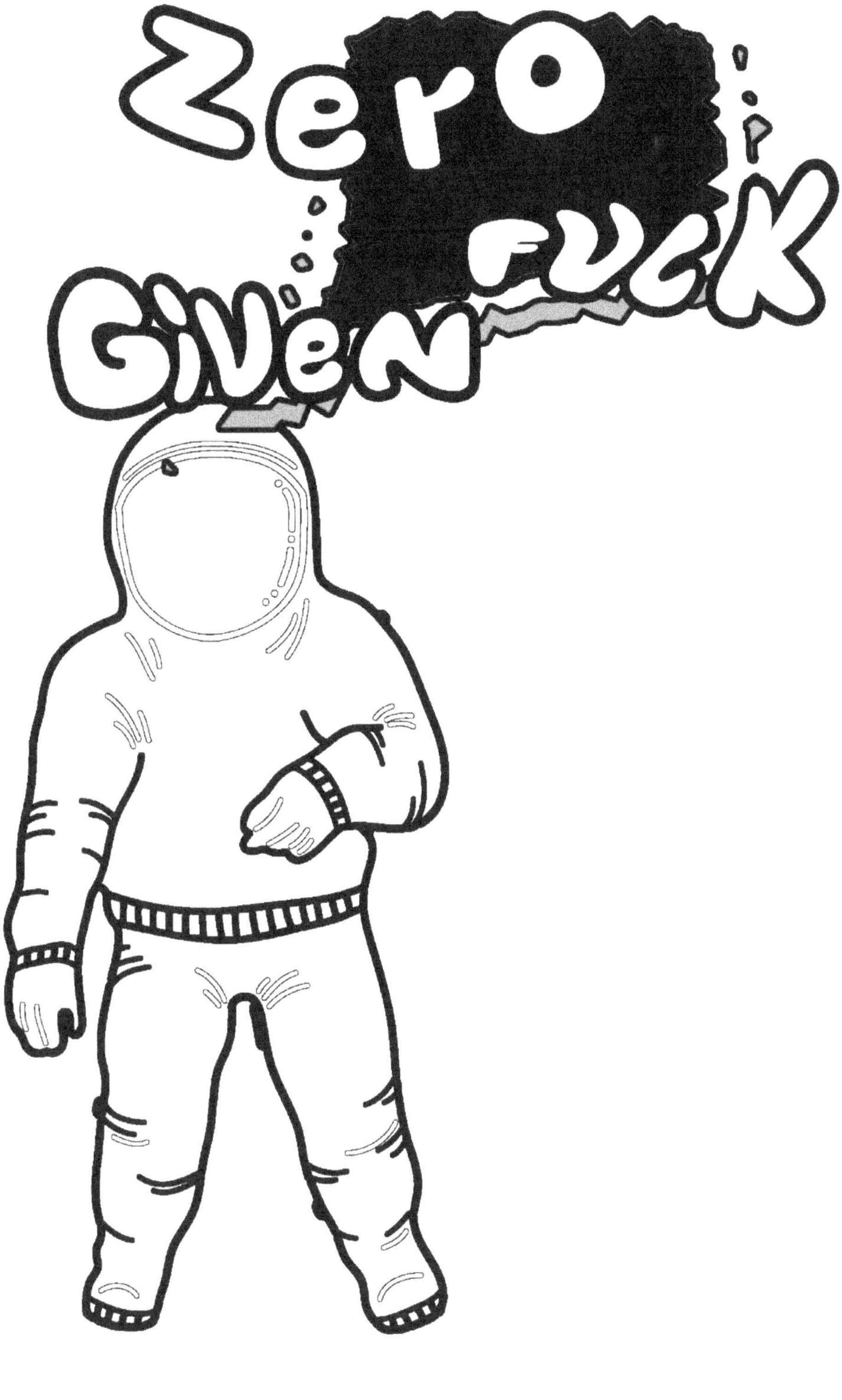
Zero
FUCK
Given

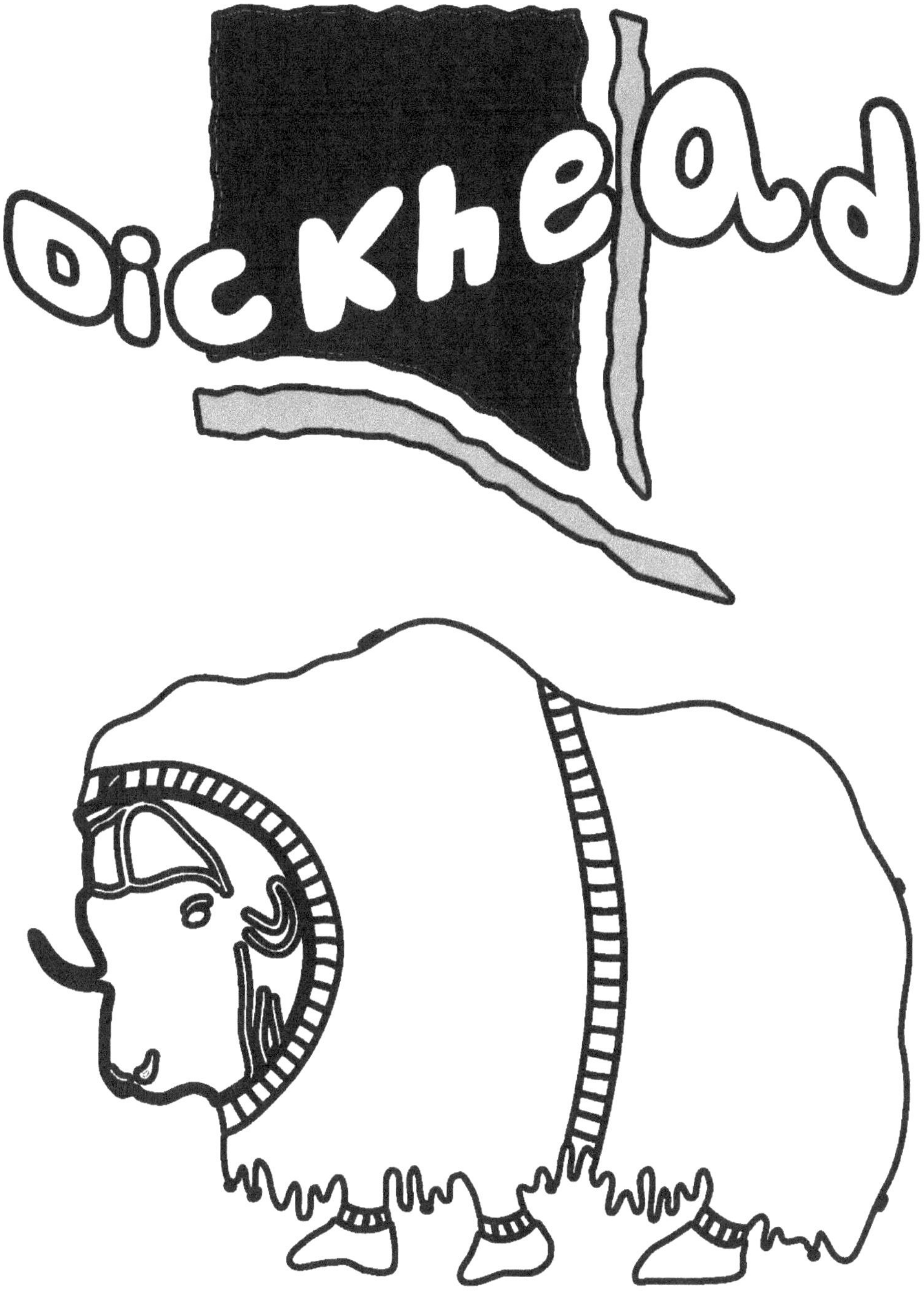
Dickhead

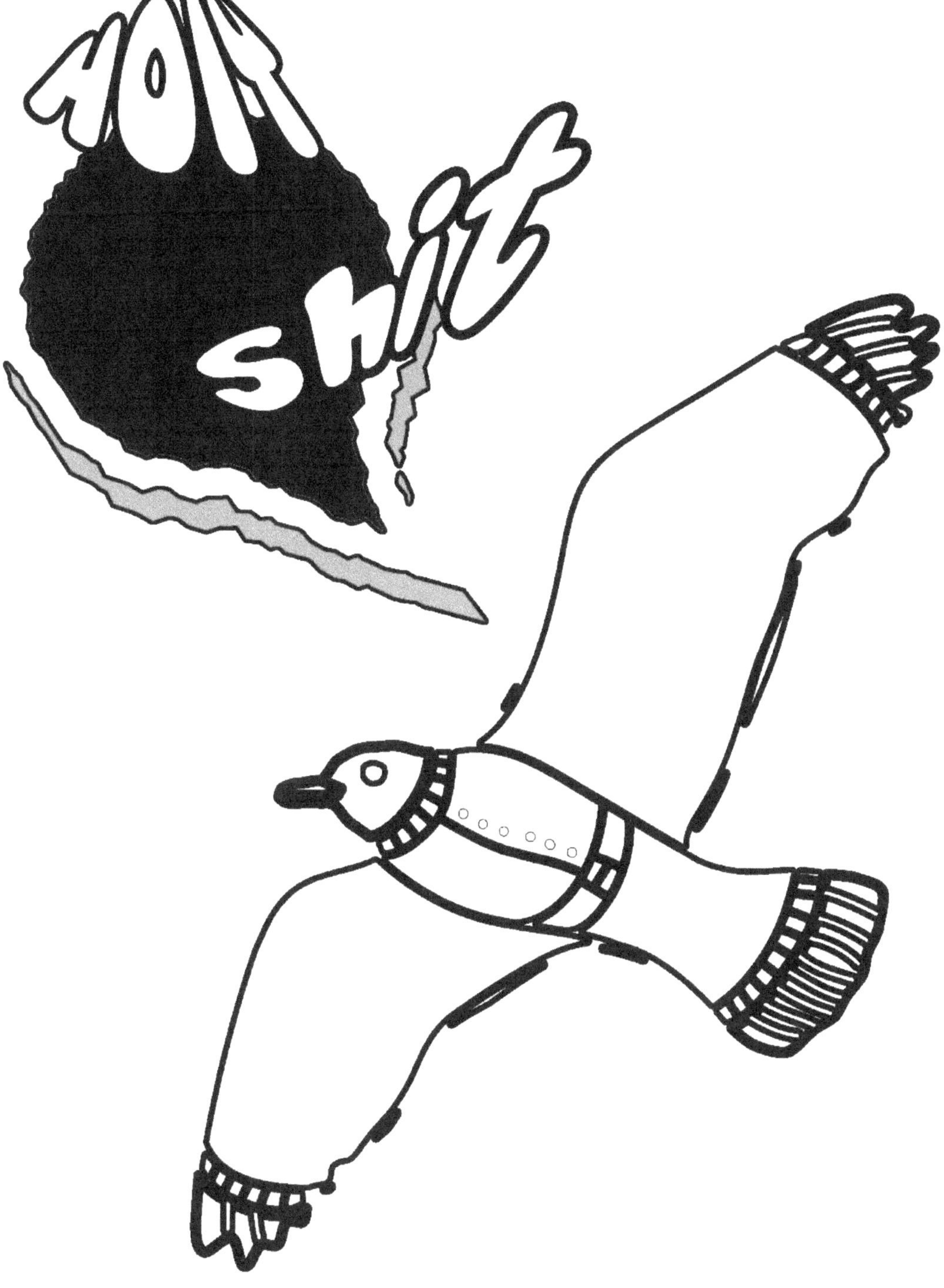
HOLY
shit

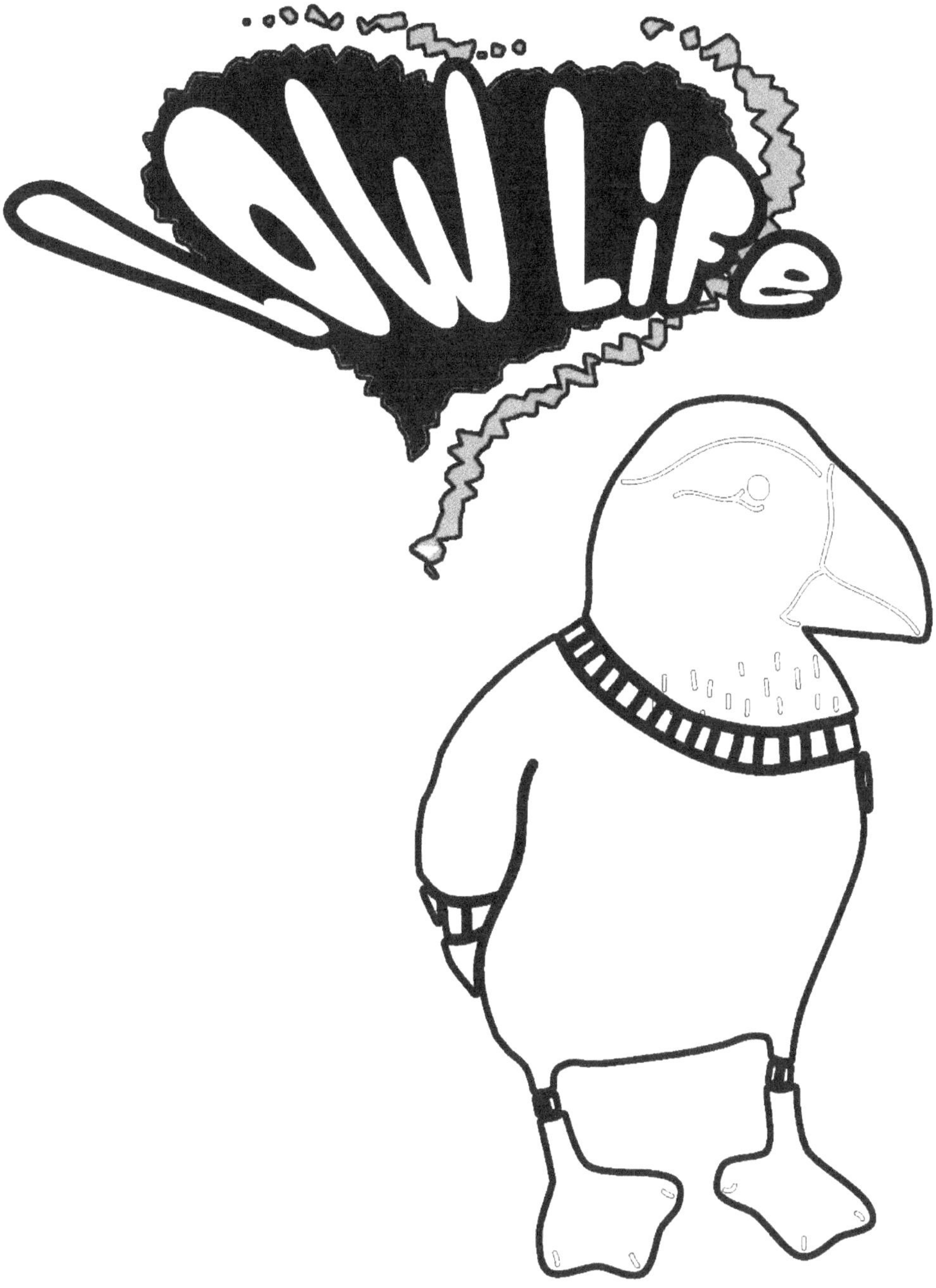
low Life

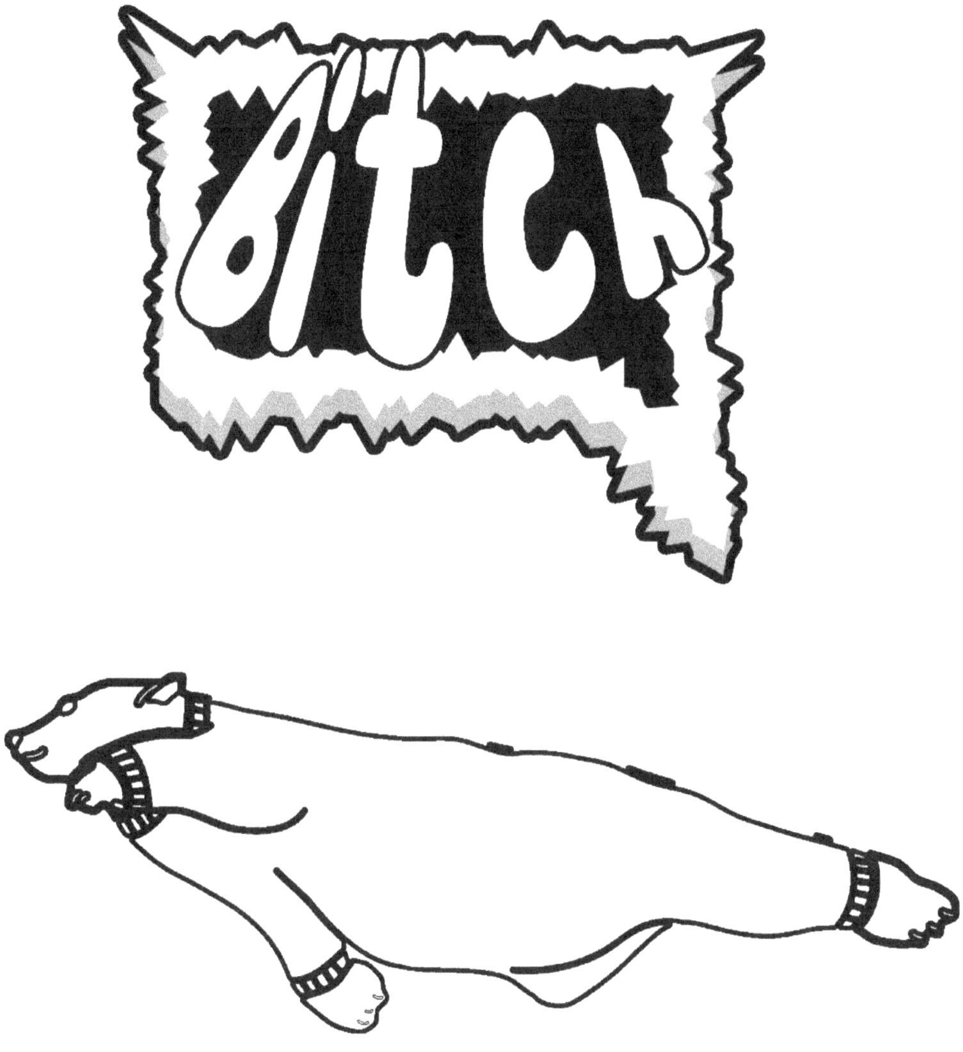
Bitch

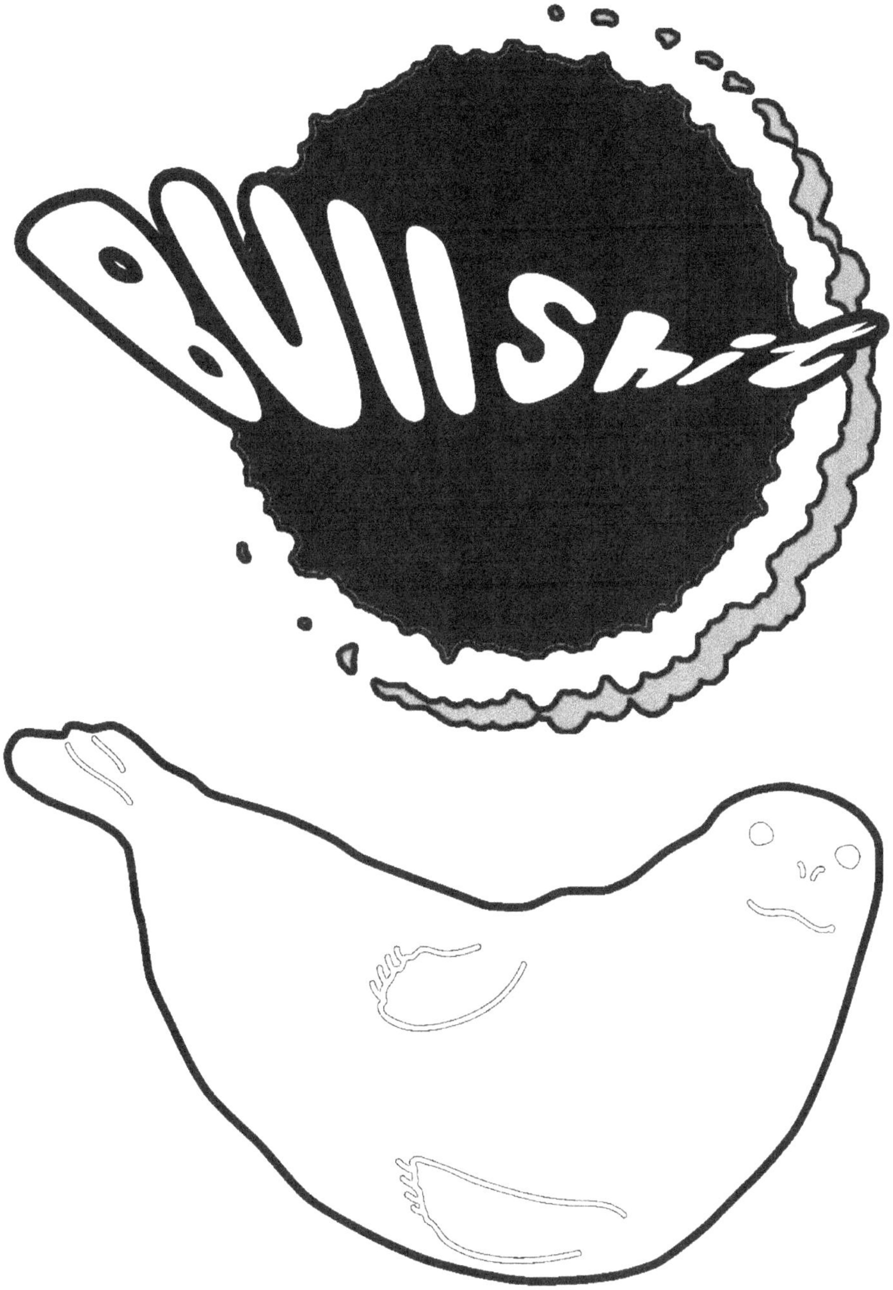

BULLshit

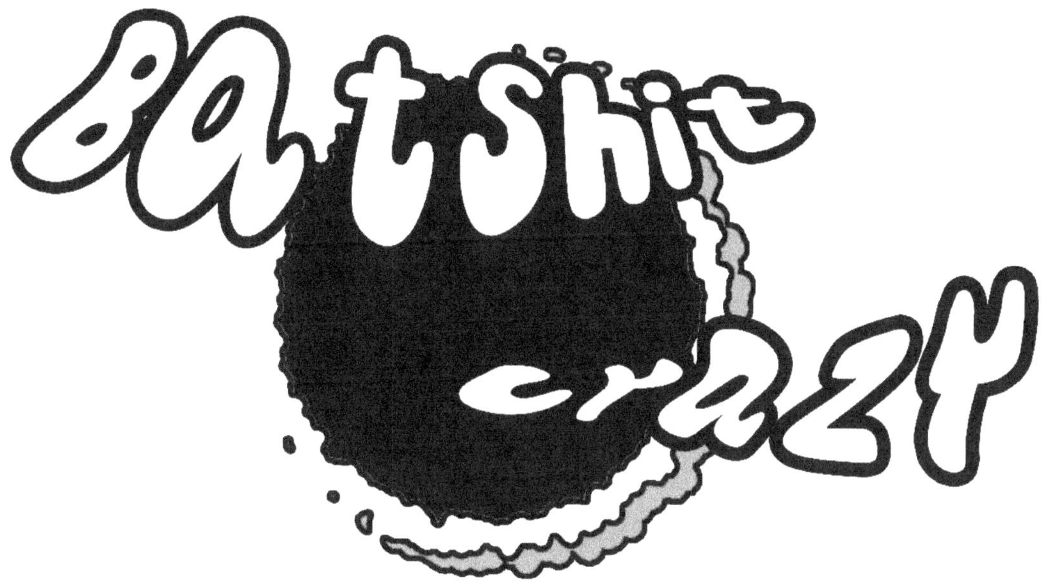
BAtShit
crAZY

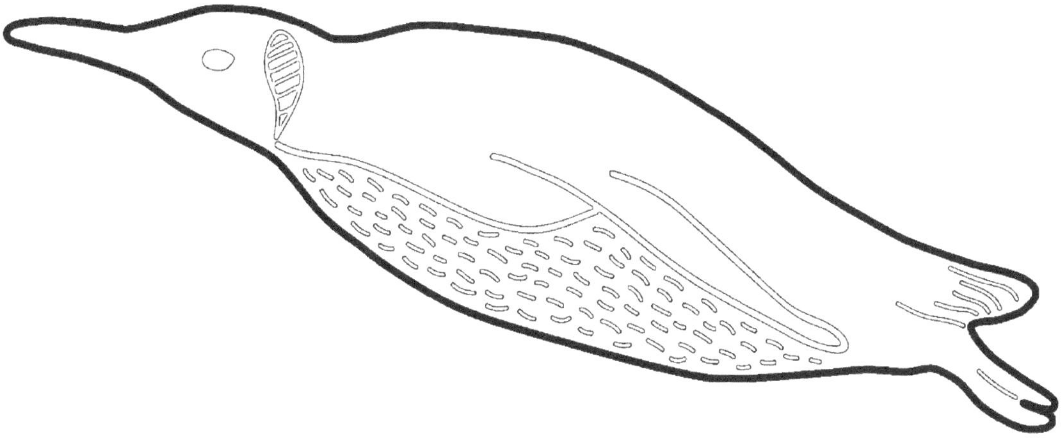

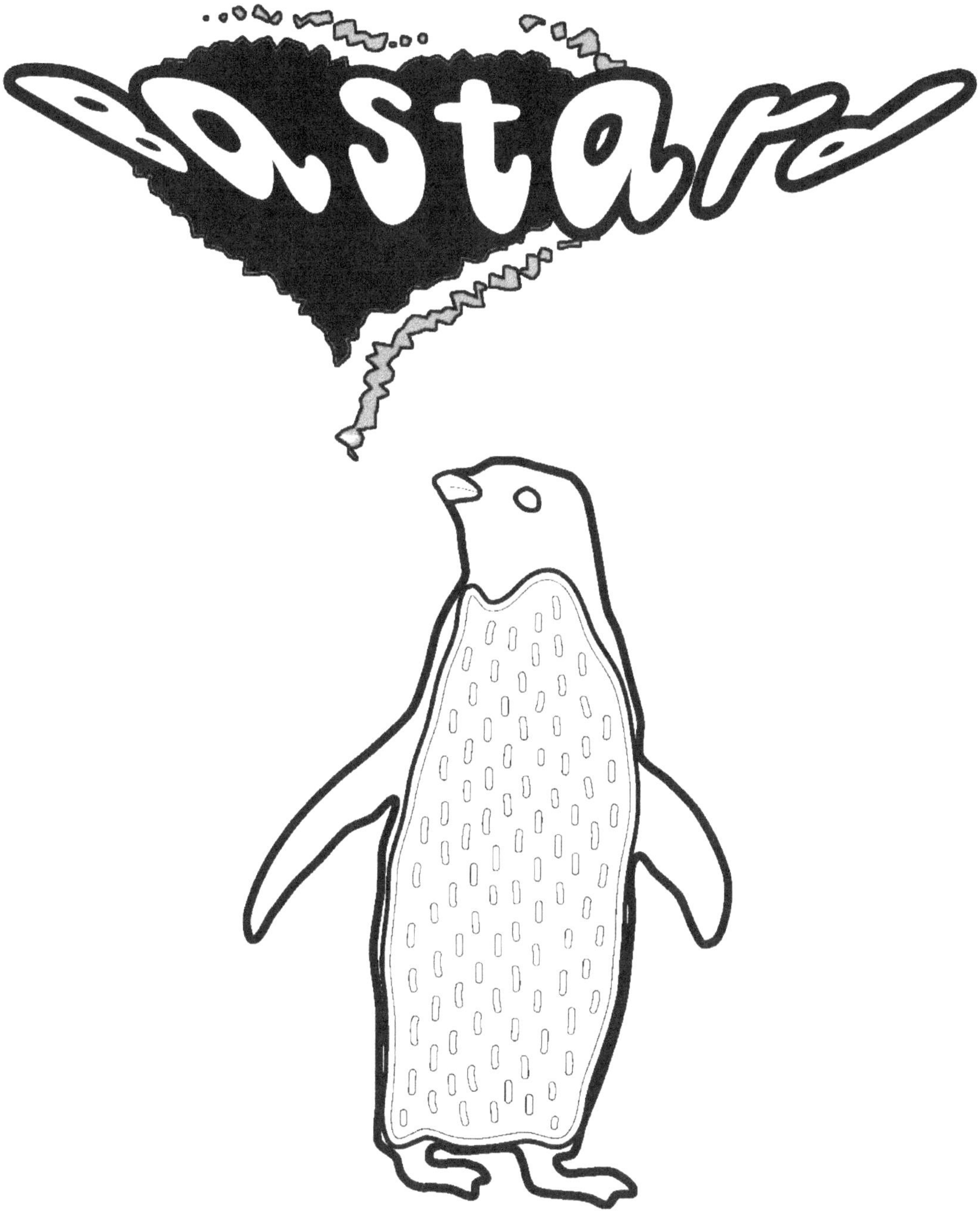
bastard

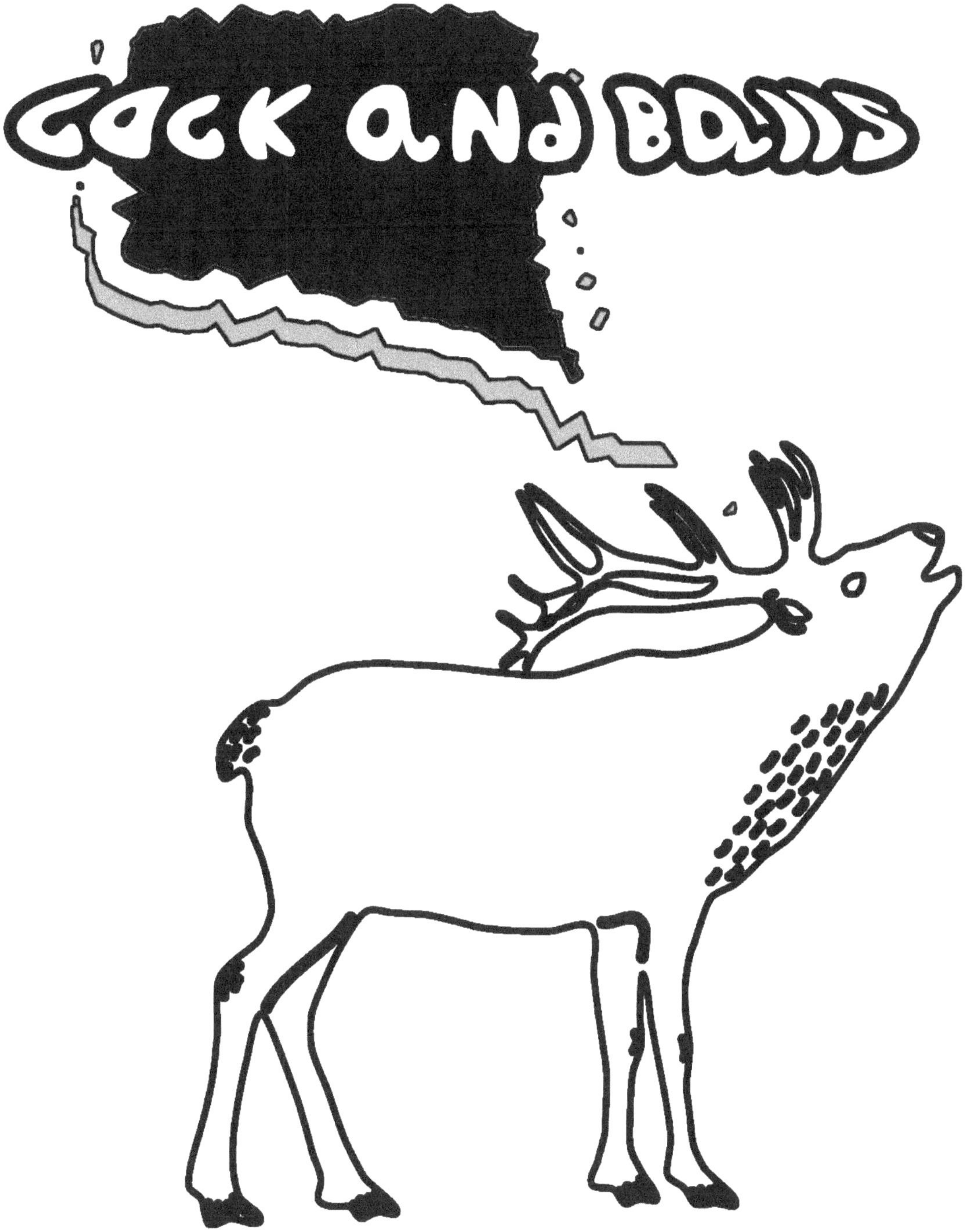
COCK AND BALLS

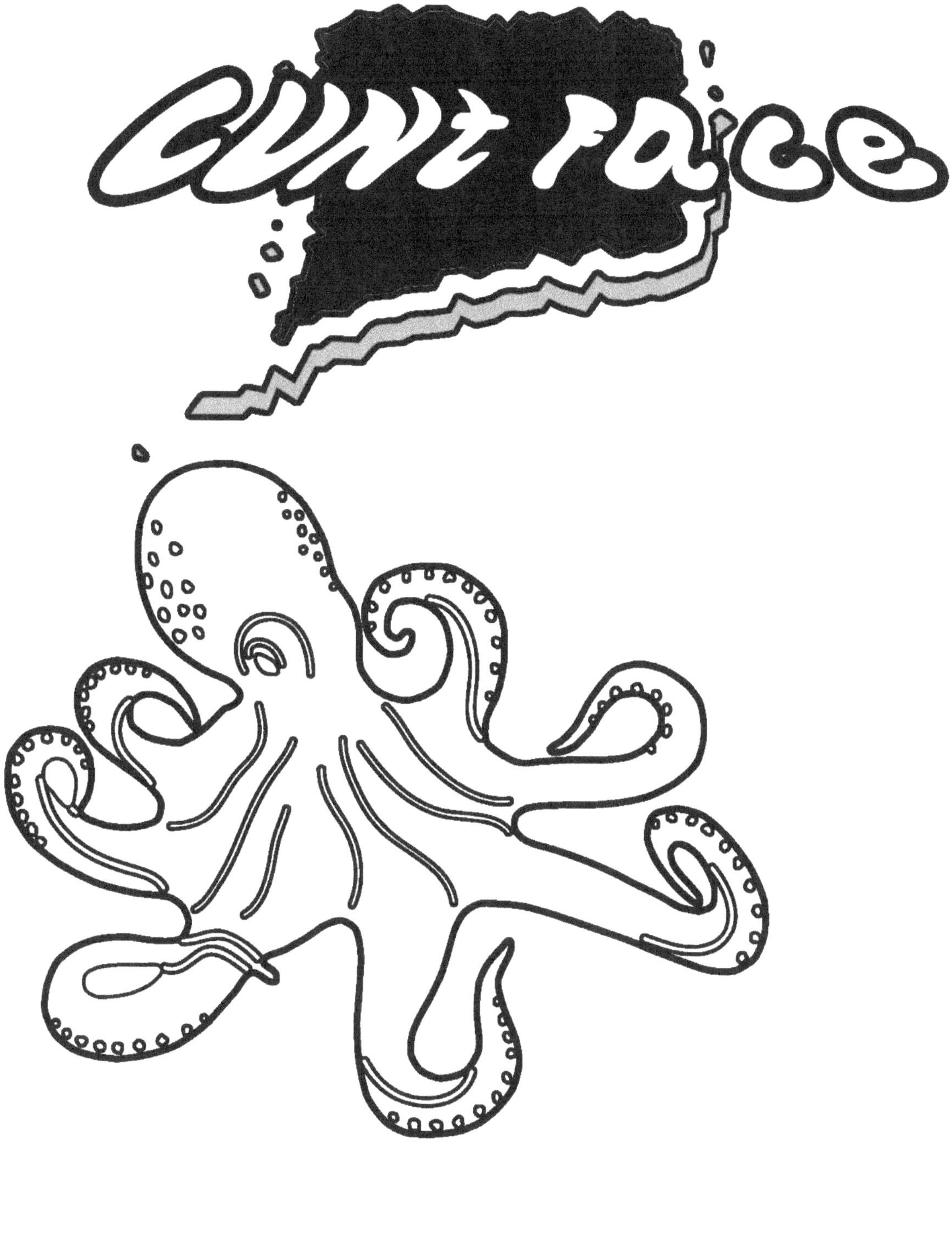
CUNT FACE

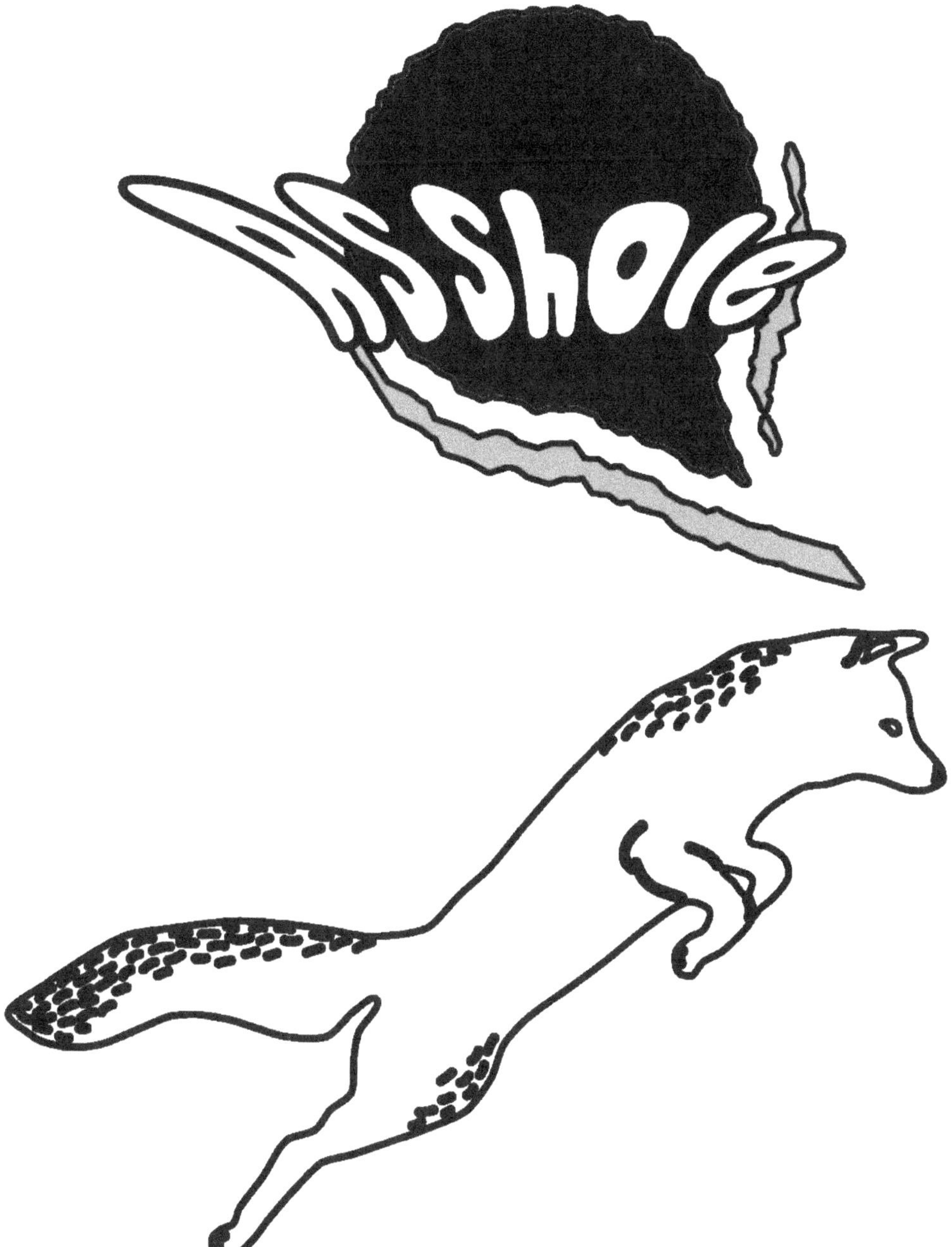
asshole

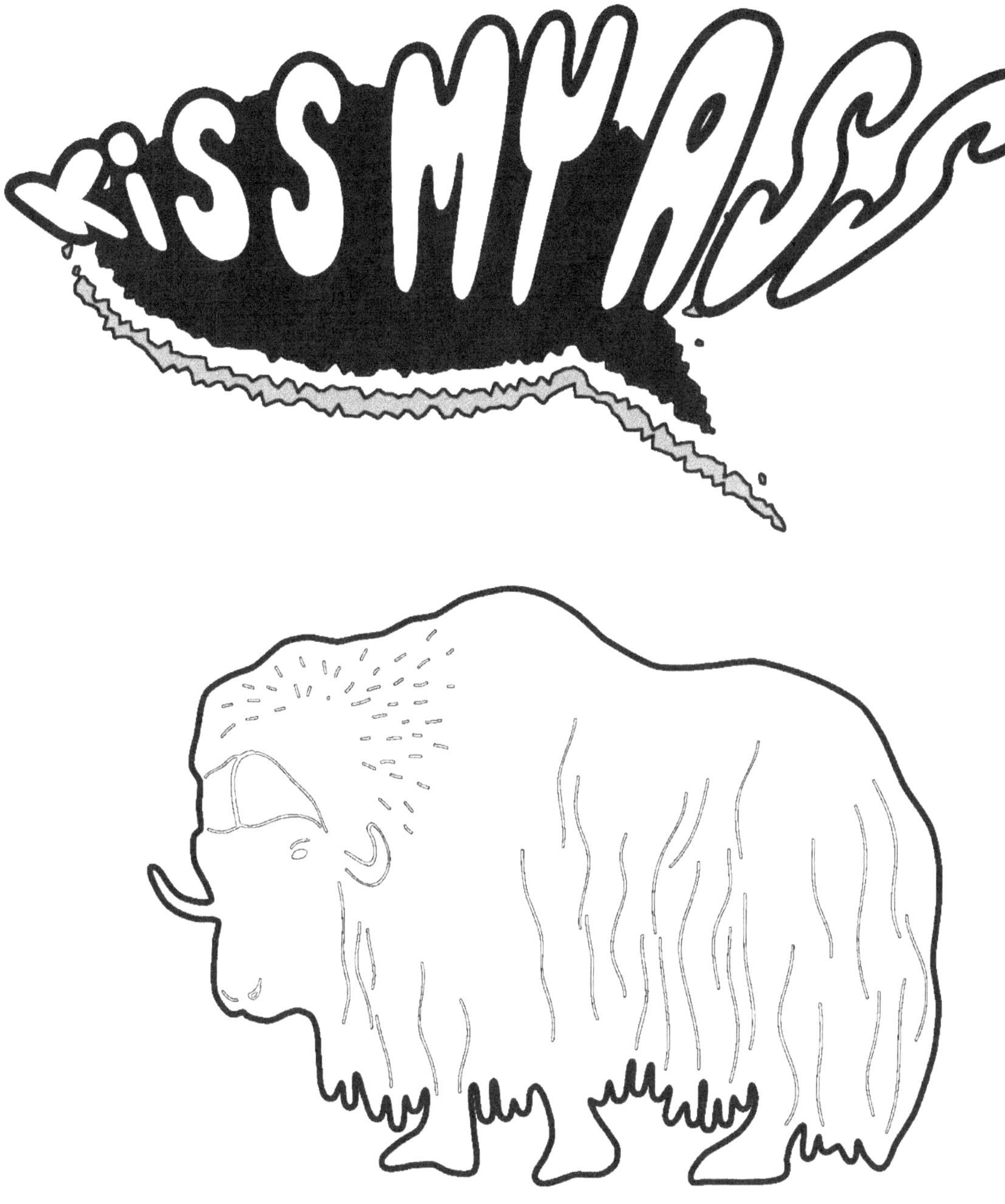
KiSS MY ASS

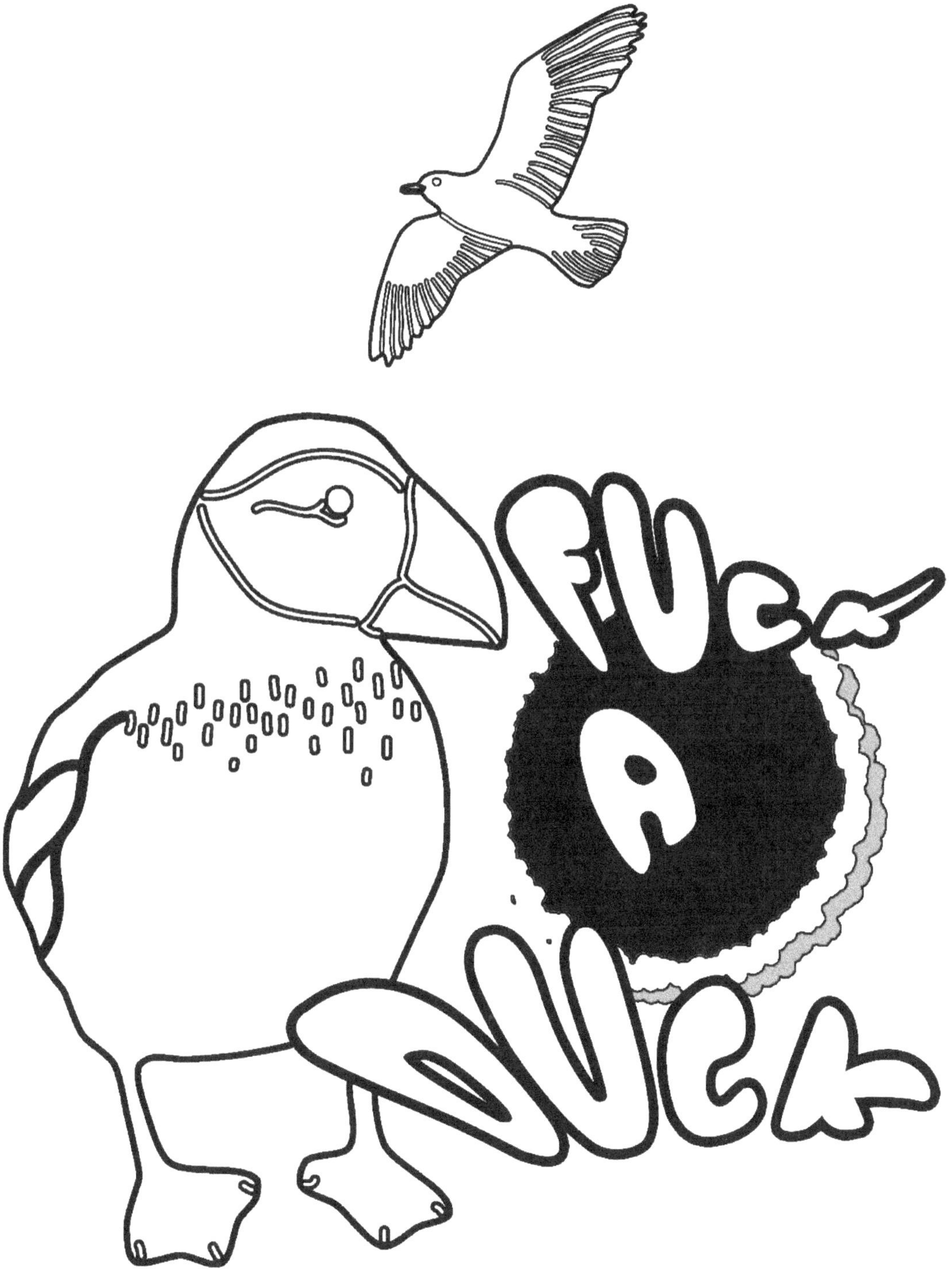
FUCK
A
DUCK

Note

www.ingramcontent.com/pod-product-compliance
Lightning Source LLC
Chambersburg PA
CBHW081122180526
45170CB00008B/2965
9781540762580